The Hávamál

The Hávamál

Saemund Sigfusson

DELFOS
Ancient Knowledge
www.freemasonrybooks.com
© 2020 ENTREACACIAS, S.L.
ENTREACACIAS, SL
[Publishing House]
Palacio Valdés, 3-5, 1ºC
33002 Oviedo - Asturias (Spain)
Tel.: (34) 984 300 233
info@freemasonrybooks.com
First edition: July, 2020

The Hávamál

The Words of

Odin

DELFOS
Ancient Knowledge

Contents

Wisdom for Wanderers and Counsel to Guests

1.

At every door-way,
ere one enters,
one should spy round,
one should pry round
for uncertain is the witting
that there be no foeman sitting,
within, before one on the floor

2.

Hail, ye Givers! a guest is come;
say! where shall he sit within?
Much pressed is he who fain on the hearth
would seek for warmth and weal.

3.

He hath need of fire, who now is come,
numbed with cold to the knee;
food and clothing the wanderer craves
who has fared o'er the rimy fell.

4.

He craves for water, who comes for refreshment,
drying and friendly bidding,
marks of good will, fair fame if 'tis won,
and welcome once and again.

5.

He hath need of his wits who wanders wide,
aught simple will serve at home;

but a gazing-stock is the fool who sits
mid the wise, and nothing knows.

6.

Let no man glory in the greatness of his mind,
but rather keep watch o'er his wits.
Cautious and silent let him enter a dwelling;
to the heedful comes seldom harm,
for none can find a more faithful friend
than the wealth of mother wit.

7.

Let the wary stranger who seeks refreshment
keep silent with sharpened hearing;
with his ears let him listen, and look with his eyes;
thus each wise man spies out the way.

8.

Happy is he who wins for himself
fair fame and kindly words;
but uneasy is that which a man doth own
while it lies in another's breast.

9.

Happy is he who hath in himself
praise and wisdom in life;
for oft doth a man ill counsel get
when 'tis born in another's breast.

10.

A better burden can no man bear

on the way than his mother wit;
'tis the refuge of the poor, and richer it seems
than wealth in a world untried.

11.

A better burden can no man bear
on the way than his mother wit:
and no worse provision can he carry with him
than too deep a draught of ale.

12.

Less good than they say for the sons of men
is the drinking oft of ale:
for the more they drink, the less can they think
and keep a watch o'er their wits.

13.

A bird of Unmindfulness flutters o'er ale feasts,
wiling away men's wits:
with the feathers of that fowl I was fettered once
in the garths of Gunnlos below.

14.

Drunk was I then, I was over drunk
in that crafty Jötun's court.
But best is an ale feast when man is able
to call back his wits at once.

15.

Silent and thoughtful and bold in strife
the prince's bairn should be.

Joyous and generous let each man show him
until he shall suffer death.

16.

A coward believes he will ever live
if he keep him safe from strife:
but old age leaves him not long in peace
though spears may spare his life.

17.

A fool will gape when he goes to a friend,
and mumble only, or mope;
but pass him the ale cup and all in a moment
the mind of that man is shown.

18.

He knows alone who has wandered wide,
and far has fared on the way,
what manner of mind a man doth own
who is wise of head and heart.

19.

Keep not the mead cup but drink thy measure;
speak needful words or none:
none shall upbraid thee for lack of breeding
if soon thou seek'st thy rest.

20.

A greedy man, if he be not mindful,
eats to his own life's hurt:

oft the belly of the fool will bring him to scorn
when he seeks the circle of the wise.

21.

Herds know the hour of their going home
and turn them again from the grass;
but never is found a foolish man
who knows the measure of his maw.

22.

The miserable man and evil minded
makes of all things mockery,
and knows not that which he best should know,
that he is not free from faults.

23.

The unwise man is awake all night,
and ponders everything over;
when morning comes he is weary in mind,
and all is a burden as ever.

24.

The unwise man weens all who smile
and flatter him are his friends,
nor notes how oft they speak him ill
when he sits in the circle of the wise.

25.

The unwise man weens all who smile
and flatter him are his friends;

but when he shall come into court he shall find
there are few to defend his cause.

26.

The unwise man thinks all to know,
while he sits in a sheltered nook;
but he knows not one thing, what he shall answer,
if men shall put him to proof.

27.

For the unwise man 'tis best to be mute
when he come amid the crowd,
for none is aware of his lack of wit
if he wastes not too many words;
for he who lacks wit shall never learn
though his words flow ne'er so fast.

28.

Wise he is deemed who can question well,
and also answer back:
the sons of men can no secret make
of the tidings told in their midst.

29.

Too many unstable words are spoken
by him who ne'er holds his peace;
the hasty tongue sings its own mishap
if it be not bridled in.

30.

Let no man be held as a laughing-stock,

though he come as guest for a meal:
wise enough seem many while they sit dry-skinned
and are not put to proof.

31.

A guest thinks him witty who mocks at a guest
and runs from his wrath away;
but none can be sure who jests at a meal
that he makes not fun among foes.

32.

Oft, though their hearts lean towards one another,
friends are divided at table;
ever the source of strife 'twill be,
that guest will anger guest.

33.

A man should take always his meals betimes
unless he visit a friend,
or he sits and mopes, and half famished seems,
and can ask or answer nought.

34.

Long is the round to a false friend leading,
e'en if he dwell on the way:
but though far off fared, to a faithful friend
straight are the roads and short.

35.

A guest must depart again on his way,
nor stay in the same place ever;

if he bide too long on another's bench
the loved one soon becomes loathed.

36.

One's own house is best, though small it may be;
each man is master at home;
though he have but two goats and a bark-thatched
hut
'tis better than craving a boon.

37.

One's own house is best, though small it may be,
each man is master at home;
with a bleeding heart will he beg, who must,
his meat at every meal.

38.

Let a man never stir on his road a step
without his weapons of war;
for unsure is the knowing when need shall arise
of a spear on the way without.

39.

I found none so noble or free with his food,
who was not gladdened with a gift,
nor one who gave of his gifts such store
but he loved reward, could he win it.

40.

Let no man stint him and suffer need
of the wealth he has won in life;

oft is saved for a foe what was meant for a friend,
and much goes worse than one weens.

41.
With raiment and arms shall friends gladden each
other,
so has one proved oneself;
for friends last longest, if fate be fair
who give and give again.

42.
To his friend a man should bear him as friend,
and gift for gift bestow,
laughter for laughter let him exchange,
but leasing pay for a lie.

43.
To his friend a man should bear him as friend,
to him and a friend of his;
but let him beware that he be not the friend
of one who is friend to his foe.

44.
Hast thou a friend whom thou trustest well,
from whom thou cravest good?
Share thy mind with him, gifts exchange with him,
fare to find him oft.

45.
But hast thou one whom thou trustest ill
yet from whom thou cravest good?

Thou shalt speak him fair, but falsely think,
and leasing pay for a lie.

46.

Yet further of him whom thou trusted ill,
and whose mind thou dost misdoubt;
thou shalt laugh with him but withhold thy
thought,
for gift with like gift should be paid.

47.

Young was I once, I walked alone,
and bewildered seemed in the way;
then I found me another and rich I thought me,
for man is the joy of man.

48.

Most blest is he who lives free and bold
and nurses never a grief,
for the fearful man is dismayed by aught,
and the mean one mourns over giving.

49.

My garments once I gave in the field
to two land-marks made as men;
heroes they seemed when once they were clothed;
'tis the naked who suffer shame!

50.

The pine tree wastes which is perched on the hill,
nor bark nor needles shelter it;

such is the man whom none doth love;
for what should he longer live?

51.

Fiercer than fire among ill friends
for five days love will burn;
bun anon 'tis quenched, when the sixth day comes,
and all friendship soon is spoiled.

52.

Not great things alone must one give to another,
praise oft is earned for nought;
with half a loaf and a tilted bowl
I have found me many a friend.

53.

Little the sand if little the seas,
little are minds of men,
for ne'er in the world were all equally wise,
'tis shared by the fools and the sage.

54.

Wise in measure let each man be;
but let him not wax too wise;
for never the happiest of men is he
who knows much of many things.

55.

Wise in measure should each man be;
but let him not wax too wise;

seldom a heart will sing with joy
if the owner be all too wise.

56.

Wise in measure should each man be,
but ne'er let him wax too wise:
who looks not forward to learn his fate
unburdened heart will bear.

57.

Brand kindles from brand until it be burned,
spark is kindled from spark,
man unfolds him by speech with man,
but grows over secret through silence.

58.

He must rise betimes who fain of another
or life or wealth would win;
scarce falls the prey to sleeping wolves,
or to slumberers victory in strife.

59.

He must rise betimes who hath few to serve him,
and see to his work himself;
who sleeps at morning is hindered much,
to the keen is wealth half-won.

60.

Of dry logs saved and roof-bark stored
a man can know the measure,

of fire-wood too which should last him out
quarter and half years to come.

61.

Fed and washed should one ride to court
though in garments none too new;
thou shalt not shame thee for shoes or breeks,
nor yet for a sorry steed.

62.

Like an eagle swooping over old ocean,
snatching after his prey,
so comes a man into court who finds
there are few to defend his cause.

63.

Each man who is wise and would wise be called
must ask and answer aright.
Let one know thy secret, but never a second, ~
if three a thousand shall know.

64.

A wise counselled man will be mild in bearing
and use his might in measure,
lest when he come his fierce foes among
he find others fiercer than he.

65.

Each man should be watchful and wary in speech,
and slow to put faith in a friend.

for the words which one to another speaks
he may win reward of ill.

66.

At many a feast I was far too late,
and much too soon at some;
drunk was the ale or yet unserved:
never hits he the joint who is hated.

67.

Here and there to a home I had haply been asked
had I needed no meat at my meals,
or were two hams left hanging in the house of that
friend
where I had partaken of one.

68.

Most dear is fire to the sons of men,
most sweet the sight of the sun;
good is health if one can but keep it,
and to live a life without shame.

69.

Not reft of all is he who is ill,
for some are blest in their bairns,
some in their kin and some in their wealth,
and some in working well.

70.

More blest are the living than the lifeless,
'tis the living who come by the cow;

I saw the hearth-fire burn in the rich man's hall
and himself lying dead at the door.

71.

The lame can ride horse, the handless drive cattle,
the deaf one can fight and prevail,
'tis happier for the blind than for him on the bale-
fire,
but no man hath care for a corpse.

72.

Best have a son though he be late born
and before him the father be dead:
seldom are stones on the wayside raised
save by kinsmen to kinsmen.

73.

Two are hosts against one, the tongue is the head's
bane,
'neath a rough hide a hand may be hid;
he is glad at nightfall who knows of his lodging,
short is the ship's berth,
and changeful the autumn night,
much veers the wind ere the fifth day
and blows round yet more in a month.

74.

He that learns nought will never know
how one is the fool of another,
for if one be rich another is poor
and for that should bear no blame.

75.

Cattle die and kinsmen die,
thyself too soon must die,
but one thing never, I ween, will die, ~
fair fame of one who has earned.

76.

Cattle die and kinsmen die,
thyself too soon must die,
but one thing never, I ween, will die, ~
the doom on each one dead.

77.

Full-stocked folds had the Fatling's sons,
who bear now a beggar's staff:
brief is wealth, as the winking of an eye,
most faithless ever of friends.

78.

If haply a fool should find for himself
wealth or a woman's love,
pride waxes in him but wisdom never
and onward he fares in his folly.

79.

All will prove true that thou askest of runes ~
those that are come from the gods,
which the high Powers wrought, and which Odin
painted:
then silence is surely best.

Maxims for All Men

80.

Praise day at even, a wife when dead,
a weapon when tried, a maid when married,
ice when 'tis crossed, and ale when 'tis drunk.

81.

Hew wood in wind, sail the seas in a breeze,
woo a maid in the dark, ~ for day's eyes are many, ~
work a ship for its gliding, a shield for its shelter,
a sword for its striking, a maid for her kiss;

82.

Drink ale by the fire, but slide on the ice;
buy a steed when 'tis lanky, a sword when 'tis rusty;
feed thy horse neath a roof, and thy hound in the
yard.

83.

The speech of a maiden should no man trust
nor the words which a woman says;
for their hearts were shaped on a whirling wheel
and falsehood fixed in their breasts.

84.

Breaking bow, or flaring flame,
ravening wolf, or croaking raven,
routing swine, or rootless tree,
waxing wave, or seething cauldron,

85.

flying arrows, or falling billow,

ice of a nighttime, coiling adder,
woman's bed-talk, or broken blade,
play of bears or a prince's child,

86.

sickly calf or self-willed thrall,
witch's flattery, new-slain foe,
brother's slayer, though seen on the highway,
half burned house, or horse too swift ~
be never so trustful as these to trust.

87.

Let none put faith in the first sown fruit
nor yet in his son too soon;
whim rules the child, and weather the field,
each is open to chance.

88.

Like the love of women whose thoughts are lies
is the driving un-roughshod o'er slippery ice
of a two year old, ill-tamed and gay;
or in a wild wind steering a helmless ship,
or the lame catching reindeer in the rime-thawed
fell.

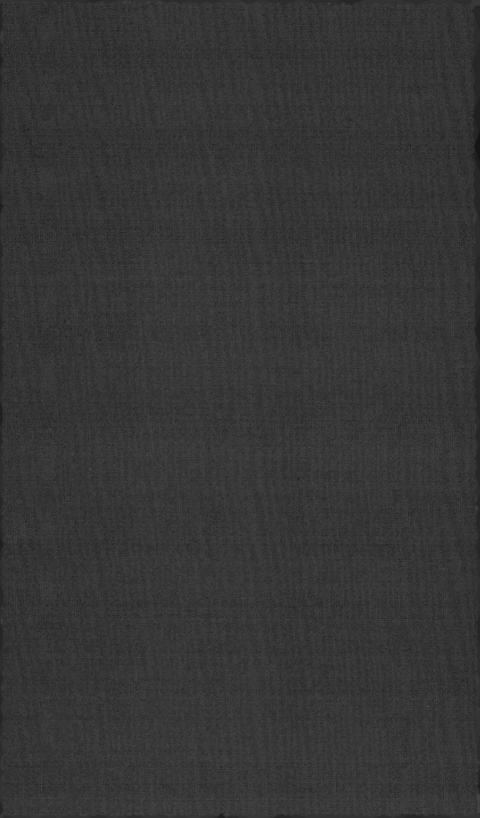

Lessons for Lovers

89.

Now plainly I speak, since both I have seen;
unfaithful is man to maid;
we speak them fairest when thoughts are falsest
and wile the wisest of hearts.

90.

~ Let him speak soft words and offer wealth
who longs for a woman's love,
praise the shape of the shining maid ~
he wins who thus doth woo.

91.

~ Never a whit should one blame another
whom love hath brought into bonds:
oft a witching form will fetch the wise
which holds not the heart of fools.

92.

Never a whit should one blame another
for a folly which many befalls;
the might of love makes sons of men
into fools who once were wise.

93.

The mind knows alone what is nearest the heart
and sees where the soul is turned:
no sickness seems to the wise so sore
as in nought to know content.

Odin's Love Quests

94.

This once I felt when I sat without
in the reeds, and looked for my love;
body and soul of me was that sweet maiden
yet never I won her as wife.

95.

Billing's daughter I found on her bed,
fairer than sunlight sleeping,
and the sweets of lordship seemed to me nought,
save I lived with that lovely form.

96.

"Yet nearer evening come thou, Odin,
if thou wilt woo a maiden:
all were undone save two knew alone
such a secret deed of shame."

97.

So away I turned from my wise intent,
and deemed my joy assured,
for all her liking and all her love
I weened that I yet should win.

98.

When I came ere long the war troop bold
were watching and waking all:
with burning brands and torches borne
they showed me my sorrowful way.

99.

Yet nearer morning I went, once more, ~
the housefolk slept in the hall,
but soon I found a barking dog
tied fast to that fair maid's couch.

100.

Many a sweet maid when one knows her mind
is fickle found towards men:
I proved it well when that prudent lass
I sought to lead astray:
shrewd maid, she sought me with every insult
and I won therewith no wife.

Odin's Quest after the Song Mead

101.

In thy home be joyous and generous to guests
discreet shalt thou be in thy bearing,
mindful and talkative, wouldst thou gain wisdom,
oft making me mention of good.
He is "Simpleton" named who has nought to say,
for such is the fashion of fools.

102.

I sought that old Jötun, now safe am I back,
little served my silence there;
but whispering many soft speeches I won
my desire in Suttung's halls.

103.

I bored me a road there with Rati's tusk
and made room to pass through the rock;
while the ways of the Jötuns stretched over and
under,
I dared my life for a draught.

104.

'Twas Gunnlod who gave me on a golden throne
a draught of the glorious mead,
but with poor reward did I pay her back
for her true and troubled heart.

105.

In a wily disguise I worked my will;
little is lacking to the wise,

for the Soul-stirrer now, sweet Mead of Song,
is brought to men's earthly abode.

106.

I misdoubt me if ever again I had come
from the realms of the Jötun race,
had I not served me of Gunnlod, sweet woman,
her whom I held in mine arms.

107.

Came forth, next day, the dread Frost Giants,
and entered the High One's Hall:
they asked ~ was the Baleworker back mid the
Powers,
or had Suttung slain him below?

108.

A ring-oath Odin I trow had taken ~
how shall one trust his troth?
'twas he who stole the mead from Suttung,
and Gunnlod caused to weep.

The Counseling of the Stray-Singer

109.

'Tis time to speak from the Sage's Seat;
hard by the Well of Weird
I saw and was silent, I saw and pondered,
I listened to the speech of men.

110.

Of runes they spoke, and the reading of runes
was little withheld from their lips:
at the High One's hall, in the High One's hall,
I thus heard the High One say: ~

111.

I counsel thee, Stray-Singer, accept my counsels,
they will be thy boon if thou obey'st them,
they will work thy weal if thou win'st them:
rise never at nighttime, except thou art spying
or seekest a spot without.

112.

I counsel thee, Stray-Singer, accept my counsels,
they will be thy boon if thou obey'st them,
they will work thy weal if thou win'st them:
thou shalt never sleep in the arms of a sorceress,
lest she should lock thy limbs;

113.

So shall she charm that thou shalt not heed
the council, or words of the king,
nor care for thy food, or the joys of mankind,
but fall into sorrowful sleep.

114.

I counsel thee, Stray-Singer, accept my counsels,
they will be thy boon if thou obey'st them,
they will work thy weal if thou win'st them:
seek not ever to draw to thyself
in love-whispering another's wife.

115.

I counsel thee, Stray-Singer, accept my counsels,
they will be thy boon if thou obey'st them,
they will work thy weal if thou win'st them:
should thou long to fare over fell and firth
provide thee well with food.

116.

I counsel thee, Stray-Singer, accept my counsels,
they will be thy boon if thou obey'st them,
they will work thy weal if thou win'st them:
tell not ever an evil man
if misfortunes thee befall,
from such ill friend thou needst never seek
return for thy trustful mind.

117.

Wounded to death, have I seen a man
by the words of an evil woman;
a lying tongue had bereft him of life,
and all without reason of right.

118.

I counsel thee, Stray-Singer, accept my counsels,
they will be thy boon if thou obey'st them,
they will work thy weal if thou win'st them:
hast thou a friend whom thou trustest well,
fare thou to find him oft;
for with brushwood grows and with grasses high
the path where no foot doth pass.

119.

I counsel thee, Stray-Singer, accept my counsels,
they will be thy boon if thou obey'st them,
they will work thy weal if thou win'st them:
in sweet converse call the righteous to thy side,
learn a healing song while thou livest.

120.

I counsel thee, Stray-Singer, accept my counsels,
they will be thy boon if thou obey'st them,
they will work thy weal if thou win'st them:
be never the first with friend of thine
to break the bond of fellowship;
care shall gnaw thy heart if thou canst not tell
all thy mind to another.

121.

I counsel thee, Stray-Singer, accept my counsels,
they will be thy boon if thou obey'st them,
they will work thy weal if thou win'st them:
never in speech with a foolish knave
shouldst thou waste a single word.

122.

From the lips of such thou needst not look
for reward of thine own good will;
but a righteous man by praise will render thee
firm in favour and love.

123.

There is mingling in friendship when man can utter
all his whole mind to another;
there is nought so vile as a fickle tongue;
no friend is he who but flatters.

124.

I counsel thee, Stray-Singer, accept my counsels,
they will be thy boon if thou obey'st them,
they will work thy weal if thou win'st them:
oft the worst lays the best one low.

125.

I counsel thee, Stray-Singer, accept my counsels,
they will be thy boon if thou obey'st them,
they will work thy weal if thou win'st them:
be not a shoemaker nor yet a shaft maker
save for thyself alone:
let the shoe be misshapen, or crooked the shaft,
and a curse on thy head will be called.

126.

I counsel thee, Stray-Singer, accept my counsels,
they will be thy boon if thou obey'st them,

they will work thy weal if thou win'st them:
when in peril thou seest thee, confess thee in peril,
nor ever give peace to thy foes.

127.

I counsel thee, Stray-Singer, accept my counsels,
they will be thy boon if thou obey'st them,
they will work thy weal if thou win'st them:
rejoice not ever at tidings of ill,
but glad let thy soul be in good.

128.

I counsel thee, Stray-Singer, accept my counsels,
they will be thy boon if thou obey'st them,
they will work thy weal if thou win'st them:
look not up in battle, when men are as beasts,
lest the wights bewitch thee with spells.

129.

I counsel thee, Stray-Singer, accept my counsels,
they will be thy boon if thou obey'st them,
they will work thy weal if thou win'st them:
wouldst thou win joy of a gentle maiden,
and lure to whispering of love,
thou shalt make fair promise, and let it be fast, ~
none will scorn their weal who can win it.

130.

I counsel thee, Stray-Singer, accept my counsels,
they will be thy boon if thou obey'st them,
they will work thy weal if thou win'st them:

I pray thee be wary, yet not too wary,
be wariest of all with ale,
with another's wife, and a third thing eke,
that knaves outwit thee never.

131.

I counsel thee, Stray-Singer, accept my counsels,
they will be thy boon if thou obey'st them,
they will work thy weal if thou win'st them:
hold not in scorn, nor mock in thy halls
a guest or wandering wight.

132.

They know but unsurely who sit within
what manner of man is come:
none is found so good, but some fault attends him,
or so ill but he serves for somewhat.

133.

I counsel thee, Stray-Singer, accept my counsels,
they will be thy boon if thou obey'st them,
they will work thy weal if thou win'st them:
hold never in scorn the hoary singer;
oft the counsel of the old is good;
come words of wisdom from the withered lips
of him left to hang among hides,
to rock with the rennets
and swing with the skins.

134.

I counsel thee, Stray-Singer, accept my counsels,

they will be thy boon if thou obey'st them,
they will work thy weal if thou win'st them:
growl not at guests, nor drive them from the gate
but show thyself gentle to the poor.

135.
Mighty is the bar to be moved away
for the entering in of all.
Shower thy wealth, or men shall wish thee
every ill in thy limbs.

136.
I counsel thee, Stray-Singer, accept my counsels,
they will be thy boon if thou obey'st them,
they will work thy weal if thou win'st them:
when ale thou quaffest, call upon earth's might ~
'tis earth drinks in the floods.
Earth prevails o'er drink, but fire o'er sickness,
the oak o'er binding, the earcorn o'er witchcraft,
the rye spur o'er rupture, the moon o'er rages,
herb o'er cattle plagues, runes o'er harm.

Odin's Quest after the Runes

137.

I trow I hung on that windy Tree
nine whole days and nights,
stabbed with a spear, offered to Odin,
myself to mine own self given,
high on that Tree of which none hath heard
from what roots it rises to heaven.

138.

None refreshed me ever with food or drink,
I peered right down in the deep;
crying aloud I lifted the Runes
then back I fell from thence.

139.

Nine mighty songs I learned from the great
son of Bale-thorn, Bestla's sire;
I drank a measure of the wondrous Mead,
with the Soulstirrer's drops I was showered.

140.

Ere long I bare fruit, and throve full well,
I grew and waxed in wisdom;
word following word, I found me words,
deed following deed, I wrought deeds.

141.

Hidden Runes shalt thou seek and interpreted
signs,
many symbols of might and power,
by the great Singer painted, by the high Powers

fashioned,
graved by the Utterer of gods.

142.

For gods graved Odin, for elves graved Daïn,
Dvalin the Dallier for dwarfs,
All-wise for Jötuns, and I, of myself,
graved some for the sons of men.

143.

Dost know how to write, dost know how to read,
dost know how to paint, dost know how to prove,
dost know how to ask, dost know how to offer,
dost know how to send, dost know how to spend?

144.

Better ask for too little than offer too much,
like the gift should be the boon;
better not to send than to overspend.
....
Thus Odin graved ere the world began;
Then he rose from the deep, and came again.

The Song of Spells

145.

Those songs I know, which nor sons of men
nor queen in a king's court knows;
the first is Help which will bring thee help
in all woes and in sorrow and strife.

146.

A second I know, which the son of men
must sing, who would heal the sick.

147.

A third I know: if sore need should come
of a spell to stay my foes;
when I sing that song, which shall blunt their
swords,
nor their weapons nor staves can wound.

148.

A fourth I know: if men make fast
in chains the joints of my limbs,
when I sing that song which shall set me free,
spring the fetters from hands and feet.

149.

A fifth I know: when I see, by foes shot,
speeding a shaft through the host,
flies it never so strongly I still can stay it,
if I get but a glimpse of its flight.

150.

A sixth I know: when some thane would harm me

in runes on a moist tree's root,
on his head alone shall light the ills
of the curse that he called upon mine.

151.

A seventh I know: if I see a hall
high o'er the bench-mates blazing,
flame it ne'er so fiercely I still can save it, ~
I know how to sing that song.

152.

An eighth I know: which all can sing
for their weal if they learn it well;
where hate shall wax 'mid the warrior sons,
I can calm it soon with that song.

153.

A ninth I know: when need befalls me
to save my vessel afloat,
I hush the wind on the stormy wave,
and soothe all the sea to rest.

154.

A tenth I know: when at night the witches
ride and sport in the air,
such spells I weave that they wander home
out of skins and wits bewildered.

155.

An eleventh I know: if haply I lead
my old comrades out to war,

I sing 'neath the shields, and they fare forth
mightily
safe into battle,
safe out of battle,
and safe return from the strife.

156.

A twelfth I know: if I see in a tree
a corpse from a halter hanging,
such spells I write, and paint in runes,
that the being descends and speaks.

157.

A thirteenth I know: if the new-born son
of a warrior I sprinkle with water,
that youth will not fail when he fares to war,
never slain shall he bow before sword.

158.

A fourteenth I know: if I needs must number
the Powers to the people of men,
I know all the nature of gods and of elves
which none can know untaught.

159.

A fifteenth I know, which Folk-stirrer sang,
the dwarf, at the gates of Dawn;
he sang strength to the gods, and skill to the elves,
and wisdom to Odin who utters.

160.

A sixteenth I know: when all sweetness and love
I would win from some artful wench,
her heart I turn, and the whole mind change
of that fair-armed lady I love.

161.

A seventeenth I know: so that e'en the shy maiden
is slow to shun my love.

162.

These songs, Stray-Singer, which man's son knows
not,
long shalt thou lack in life,
though thy weal if thou win'st them, thy boon if
thou obey'st them
thy good if haply thou gain'st them.

163.

An eighteenth I know: which I ne'er shall tell
to maiden or wife of man
save alone to my sister, or haply to her
who folds me fast in her arms;
most safe are secrets known to but one-
the songs are sung to an end.

164.

Now the sayings of the High One are uttered in the
hall
for the weal of men, for the woe of Jötuns,
Hail, thou who hast spoken! Hail, thou that

knowest!
Hail, ye that have hearkened! Use, thou who hast
learned!

Made in the USA
Middletown, DE
05 November 2024

63943541R00045